Seeded Light

Seeded Light

Poems by Edward Byrne

Turning Point

© 2010 by Edward Byrne

Published by Turning Point
P.O. Box 541106
Cincinnati, OH 45254-1106

ISBN: 9781934999783
LCCN: 2009942080

Poetry Editor: Kevin Walzer
Business Editor: Lori Jareo

Visit us on the web at www.turningpointbooks.com

Acknowledgments

Grateful acknowledgment is made to the editors and institutional sponsors of the following journals or anthologies in which these poems first appeared, although often in a different version or under another title.

Journals:

Adirondack Review: "Rafting the Rapids"; *American Literary Review*: "Lightning Strike"; *Blue Mesa Review*: "Coronary Thrombosis"; *Blueline*: "Winter Waters: White Mountains, New Hampshire"; *Borderlands: Texas Poetry Review*: "Returning to Your Father's Farm"; *Canary River Review*: "Rainbow over Snow-Covered Landscape" and "Revision by Lamplight"; *Center: A Journal of the Literary Arts*: "After the Miscarriage" and "Church Burning"; *Cimarron Review*: "Waiting at a Bus Station"; *Clackamas Literary Review*: "Anniversary Visit" and "Spring Morning: Descending an Abandoned Mountain"; *Connecticut Review*: "Thanksgiving: Before Leaving for Home"; *Crab Orchard Review*: "Listening to Lester Young"; *Cresset*: "Spring Sunset: Learning About the Death of a Friend" [as "Spring Sunset: Upon Learning About the Death of a Friend"]; *Descant*: "Winter Scene: After the Aneurysm"; *Ekphrasis*: "Summer Evening: Truro, 1947"; *Ellipsis Magazine*: "Sailing into the Storm"; *Evansville Review*: "Winter Nightfall in a Seaside Village" [as "Five Stanzas in Winter"]; *Florida Review*: "Triptych: Fly-by over the Wildlife Refuge"; *Greensboro Review*: "Moonlight in the City"; *James Dickey Newsletter*: "Nocturnal: Fayette County, West Virginia"; *The Literary Review*: "After Leaving the Hotel" and "Night Vision"; *Midland Review*: "Moonrise over the River"; *Natural Bridge*: "Cross Sections: Notes from a Memoir"; *New Delta Review*: "Wyoming Elegy"; *North American Review*: "Curacao: Notes from a Summer Memoir"; *Quarterly West*: "Fault Line: A Farewell in Five Fragments"; *River Oak Review*: "Easter Weekend: Sunrise by the Bay"; *South Coast Poetry Journal*: "Awaiting the Afternoon Rain"; *South Dakota Review*: "Constellations over

Colorado"; *Southern Poetry Review*: "Solitude: A Meditation in Four Fragments" [as "Solitude: A Meditation in Four Fragments (After Keats)"]; *Sycamore Review*: "Wharf at Sunset: A Sketch" [as "Wharf at Sunset"]; *Tar River Poetry*: "Canyon Tributary*"*; *The Wallace Stevens Journal*: "Invoking a Line by Wallace Stevens"; *Weber Studies*: "Leaving Lisbon After a Lengthy Visit" and "Mountain Meadow: Night Climb After a Storm."

Anthologies:

"Envying the Art of the Cartographer" appeared in an anthology, *Red, White, & Blues: Poetic Vistas on the Promise of America*, published by the University of Iowa Press. "Listening to Lester Young" appeared in an anthology, *The Book of Irish American Poetry from the Eighteenth Century to the Present*, published by the University of Notre Dame Press. "Nightfall After a Storm" appeared in an anthology, *The Sacred Place: Witnessing the Holy in the Physical World*, published by the University of Utah Press. "Leaving Lisbon After a Lengthy Visit" appeared in an anthology special issue of *Gaia: Literary and Environmental Arts*; "Winter Scene: After the Aneurysm" [as "Winter Scene"] appeared in an anthology, *A Poetic Vision*, published by the Brauer Museum of Art and the Valparaiso University Department of English.

For Pam and Alex

Table of Contents

1. Night Vision

Moonlight in the City..15
Waiting at a Bus Station...17
Church Burning..19
Anniversary Visit...21
Returning to Your Father's Farm..........................22
After the Miscarriage..24
Night Vision..26
Thanksgiving: Before Leaving for Home............28

2. Sailing into the Storm

Curacao: Notes from a Summer Memoir............33
Wharf at Sunset: A Sketch.....................................34
Triptych: Fly-by over the Wildlife Refuge...........36
Sailing into the Storm...38
Leaving Lisbon After a Lengthy Visit..................40
Rainbow over Snow-Covered Landscape............41
Winter Nightfall in a Seaside Village 43
Easter Weekend: Sunrise by the Bay....................44

3. Fault Line

Revision by Lamplight..49
Envying the Art of the Cartographer...................50
Moonrise over the River...53
Nocturnal: Fayette County, West Virginia...........55
Awaiting the Afternoon Rain.................................56
Lightning Strike...57
Winter Waters: White Mountains,
 New Hampshire..59
Fault Line: A Farewell in Five Fragments.............62

4. Constellations over Colorado

Canyon Tributary..67
Mountain Meadow: Night Climb
    After a Storm...69
Spring Morning: Descending an Abandoned
    Mountain..70
Winter Scene: After the Aneurysm......................71
Wyoming Elegy...73
After Leaving the Hotel.......................................75
Constellations over Colorado...............................78
Listening to Lester Young....................................81

5. Rafting the Rapids

Invoking a Line by Wallace Stevens......................87
Spring Sunset: Learning About the Death
    of a Friend..88
Summer Evening: Truro, 1947..............................90
Cross Sections: Notes from a Memoir..................93
Rafting the Rapids...96
Coronary Thrombosis...98
Solitude: A Meditation in Four Fragments.........100
Nightfall After a Storm.......................................102

*The immense deserted night set up its formation
of colossal figures that seeded light far and wide.*

*

I could write the saddest poem tonight.

—Pablo Neruda

1. Night Vision

Moonlight in the City

One July evening when I was eleven,
        not a block from the waterfront, the day

yet hot, I waited by myself in the middle
        of a vacant lot and watched as a fresh wash

of moonlight began to flow over rooftops,
        and the sky beyond dust-covered billboards

just started to fill with clustered stars.
        The splintered grids of far-off apartment

fire escapes glittered against their backdrop
        of red brick as if lit by the flick of a switch.

In this distance, even the paired lines
        of elevated train tracks, stretching like bars

along the edge of the shore, appeared
        to shine, and those symmetrical rows

of windows on the warehouses below
        seemed almost to glow. Warning lights

pulsed all along the span of that great
        bridge over the river, as hundreds of bright

buds suddenly stippled those rippling
        waters now deepening to the blue of a new

bruise. Steel supports wound around
        one another into braided suspension cables

dipping toward either end and glinting
        beneath that constellation still slowly

showing in the darker corridor overhead.
    Already, I could see the outlines of lunar

topography, and I thought of that old
    globe my grandfather had once given me

only days before he died—of how
    I'd felt its raised beige shapes representing

the seven continents, and of the way
    he told me he'd been to every one of them.

Somewhere in the city, summertime
    sounds—the high screams of sirens

and muffled bass thumps of fireworks—
    played like the muscular backup music

pumping from some local garage band.
    But I stood listlessly under sharp-angled

shadows cast by street lamps, among
    an urban wreckage of broken cinder blocks

and glistening shards of shattered panes,
    and I listened to the wind-clank of chain-link

fencing around that grassless plot of land,
    knowing that night my father was far away

again, driving deliveries along an interstate,
    and my mother was sitting alone at home,

as were her neighbors, awaiting the first
    broadcast of a man walking on the moon.

Waiting at a Bus Station

I. *A False Warmth*

Although the traffic outside is stalled by snowfall,
    and home now appears as far away as those stars

we know are still slowly drifting in some distant
    sky, both of us wait at this bus station, hoping

the roads will soon be cleared. And though we've
    been here for more than four hours, the frozen

street scene we see through these windows, long
    gone gray with exhaust and streaked by everyday

stains, remains the same. Snowflakes flutter
    through an evening air scarred only by the thin

bare branches of those few oaks newly planted
    last spring in this city's latest urban renewal plan.

All the midtown shops have shut down for the day,
    though their neon signs and bright display cases

are yet glowing through the snow with a false
    warmth like those words and images on the pages

of any good book passing along to us lasting
    reminders of a certain time and place, or those old

family albums found in attics, so often offering
    tinted vintage photographs—sometimes blurred

by quick movements, camera lenses left out of focus—
    evidence of events important in someone else's past.

II. *A Small All-Night Diner*

Even the local pharmacist closed this afternoon,
    leaving an emergency number in oversize scrawl

on an unrolled scroll of computer printer paper
    taped like a large bandage to his storefront door.

Only that small all-night diner across the way
    has stayed open, its steamy backlit pair of frosted

windows staring back at us in an opaque glare.
    We ate a late lunch there, shared a booth with two

other stranded travelers—husband and wife,
    strangers like us, come from the east, changing

buses for a more northern course, drinking cup
    after cup of black coffee. Passing back and forth

ketchup, a salt or pepper shaker, we discussed
    the storm, watched it through fogged plate glass:

the bus station on the opposite side of the avenue,
    a couple apparently peering back from the terminal

lobby already growing bleary in windblown snow,
    everything else outside just now becoming unclear

like the distortion one might find in a hurried
    snapshot, the whole world fading away to white

as if it were nothing but a quick picture accidentally
    caught forever on someone's overexposed roll of film.

Church Burning

Nearly a year after the church burning
      our memories of the damage remain,

although only in those images we have
      chosen to retain: the first fire-bomb flash

that filled the air with ashes; soot
      that seemed to cover everyone in the color

of mourning; clouds of brown powder
      showering down as if sifted, drifting

like silt; coal-dark smoke that rose,
      floating, blown slightly downwind

with its tail trailing back, curling toward
      the steeple like a black banner unfurling

as it wavered overhead; and the blasted
      panes of stained glass, the spire's twin

windows, now sparkling on an asphalt
      parking lot like starlight on sea water.

When we tried to enter, flames came
      around the door frame, their thin flares

bending and twisting—imagine red,
      long, and slender willow twigs—in what

little wind there was. We stood watch
      all night, knowing no more than a torn

scrap of smoldering fabric, like faith,
      might reignite everything. Although a stench

of sulfur lingered until dawn, the way
    torchlight fumes sometimes may stay,

even before the scorch of morning sun
    showed over those ruins, we believed

the rebuilding would begin with daylight.
    Today, the charred parts are hardly visible

anymore, and while the white marble
    stone in the sanctuary only darkens at dusk,

as though yet lightly coated with charcoal
    dust, anyone would barely be aware there

ever had been a fire, except sometimes
    on Sundays when congregation members

remember that sharp scent of singed
    wood, which still mingles in with the incense.

Anniversary Visit

Tonight, my wife and I will arrive again at that inn
    we first visited a decade ago. Nestled into a high rise

beside the river, its balconies stretch out, as if gliding
    over the slow-flowing waters below, and in morning

their shadows will reach across to the other shore
    like black boxes stacked on an Ad Reinhardt abstract.

We will walk a path that parts the garden flowers,
    so orderly arranged with constellations of violet

and pink blossoms separated from others of red
    and yellow. We will speak once more of that week

now long gone and about those late afternoons
    when we had slept with tangled legs in a hammock

sagging under the twisting limbs of shade trees.
    We will seek out those same old signposts along

an upper trail, which yet creases the hillside, leads
    to that distant peak with its white curve of waterfall

jutting just above us. Through our field glasses,
    the geometry of far-off farmlands will appear near

and take on shapes similar to the puzzle pieces
    our son loves to fit together when we are at home.

We will look back at that cluster of cottages
    from another age still filling the village in the valley,

and of course, they'll also seem so much closer.
    And then we will pretend we are ten years younger.

Returning to Your Father's Farm

I

Except for a few scampering field mice
    and a pair of scrawny dogs scavenging

the grounds, this farm your father once
    owned now lies abandoned, its broad

fields fallow, the dark soil left unturned
    for too long, until it has become as fine

and dry as drifting dust. Overgrown
    weeds have swollen all around the red,

weathered barn, its swayed back caving
    the way even good wood gives in to age.

Shapelessly rising toward clouds, these
    trees in the windbreak appear gaunt,

their withered limbs weakly wavering
    in the light southern winds of summer.

II

Scraps of machinery and old oil drums
    stacked upon one another spot the area,

marring the large back yard where your
    grandmother's garden had been, where

as a girl you used to gather vegetables.
    At a distance, desolate meadows seem

to meander toward the wide horizon,
    and the decaying building wearing down

before us does not resemble the carefully
    kept farmhouse surrounded by straight,

full rows of crops that I had often seen
    stilled in so many family photographs.

Feeling we've lingered long enough,
    we leave, believing we'll never return again.

After the Miscarriage

Before breakfast, passing below the blank
    windows of lovers' hotel rooms, we walked

toward the harbor. At the end of a steep
    cobblestone street, we could see the water's

edge, its morning mist still lifting
    like a vague gray veil and dissipating

as if in some deliberate act of abandonment,
    although the horizon line was yet nowhere

to be seen. A few boys in black coats
    huddled together against the still chilly

spring weather. Beside the low wall
    along the wharf that now seemed bleached

white by an early light, hands cupped
    for shelter from the wind, they smoked

cigarettes and spoke of last evening's
    adventures—once more told those lies

they'd told before. Alone among rows
    of umbrellaless café tables, you wrote

notes home on a picture postcard
    addressed to your sister, while I bought

fresh fruit and flowers at the market,
    even though I could not find the yellow

roses you'd hoped would brighten
    our rented brownstone apartment.

Returning, we moved through the public
    park, its thin trees and clusters of lilac

shrubs just beginning to bud, its large
    garden plots already filling with color.

As we followed the red brick path
    all around a reflecting pool, we listened

to the shrill whistle of an overnight
    train finally arriving at the railway

terminal, and we heard the slow toll
    of cathedral bells calling parishioners

for morning Mass, both of us believing
    each sound offered its own form of warning.

Night Vision

> *What for the visions of the night? Our life is so safe*
> *and regular that we hardly know the emotion of terror....*
> *And yet dreams acquaint us with what the day omits.*
>   —Ralph Waldo Emerson

In the small park behind our home, the trees
    stand as straight and stark as upended broomsticks,

as if all day they've been sweeping clean the now
    dark and now cloudless sky. An intricate network

of branches catches the wind and some long limbs
    scratch against one another like blades of scissors

slicing a sheet of unseen paper. Tonight, awakened
    by a dream, I unwrapped myself from the intimate

sleep-twist of your body, searched the corners
    for those clothes I had thrown off in haste only

hours earlier, and staggered out, half-consciously,
    into the moonless night air blackened beyond barren

patches of garden plots and sour mulch-heaps
    that spot our yard. Alone, beside the lined practice

grounds, where all day padded boys endlessly
    toss footballs to one another, or young fathers

earnestly sail multi-colored kites above a jagged
    edge of bared treetops for their children, I reviewed

that vision I had seen in sleep. Somehow, there,
    among the stone tables and the wooden benches,

I once more felt childlike, again imagined
      the setting that had come to me in bed—the open

field, the bright sky—and pictured myself racing
      across a meadow, chasing after the fading image

of my father (outlined, as if in eclipse, against
      a strong summer sun slung low over the horizon,

just rising), the way I often would have done.
      In my dream, you were also there: lost, crying

out as if in pain (still the woman you are
      today, except three decades misplaced), unsure

which direction to travel toward home, hoping
      someone would find you, wondering who was this

boy rushing past you and where was he going.
      I, too, didn't know who you were, and never would

know. Even now, as I stand beneath these empty
      trees and this star-filled sky, I still see the agony

in your face as you seemed hurt by my going,
      and I try to explain why I couldn't help you—

I was only a child passing by, running toward
      blinding sunlight, following my father's shadow.

Thanksgiving:
Before Leaving for Home

I

At first, one row of clouds fell below that nearby
    mountain ridge and we could feel the swift wind

of winter's initial cold front suddenly sweeping
    across a gray field, still darkened by their stain,

or throwing about those leaves blowing like snow
    into drifts along the ground all around our rented

house; even today, we know there is no way this
    day will ever recede very far from our memories.

II

Not much more than a few hours earlier, you
    and I had again awakened long before morning's

sunrise, though our windows were then whitened
    by moonlight, to the sound of our young son's

cries for someone to come to him. As if those
    roaming shadows that had emerged were thieves,

he'd felt loss move through his room from dresser
    to desk to chest; an absence had already taken place.

III

Who knew the hospital would be so far away?
    Beneath black branches, wind-thinned and arching

overhead, almost as dark as those cavern walls
    we'd visited earlier in our vacation, a stark road

wound around the edge of town, coiling toward
    some distant hint of morning light just beginning

to glint up ahead; at last, with each shallow swallow
    he'd breathe, we now could see how close we were.

2. Sailing into the Storm

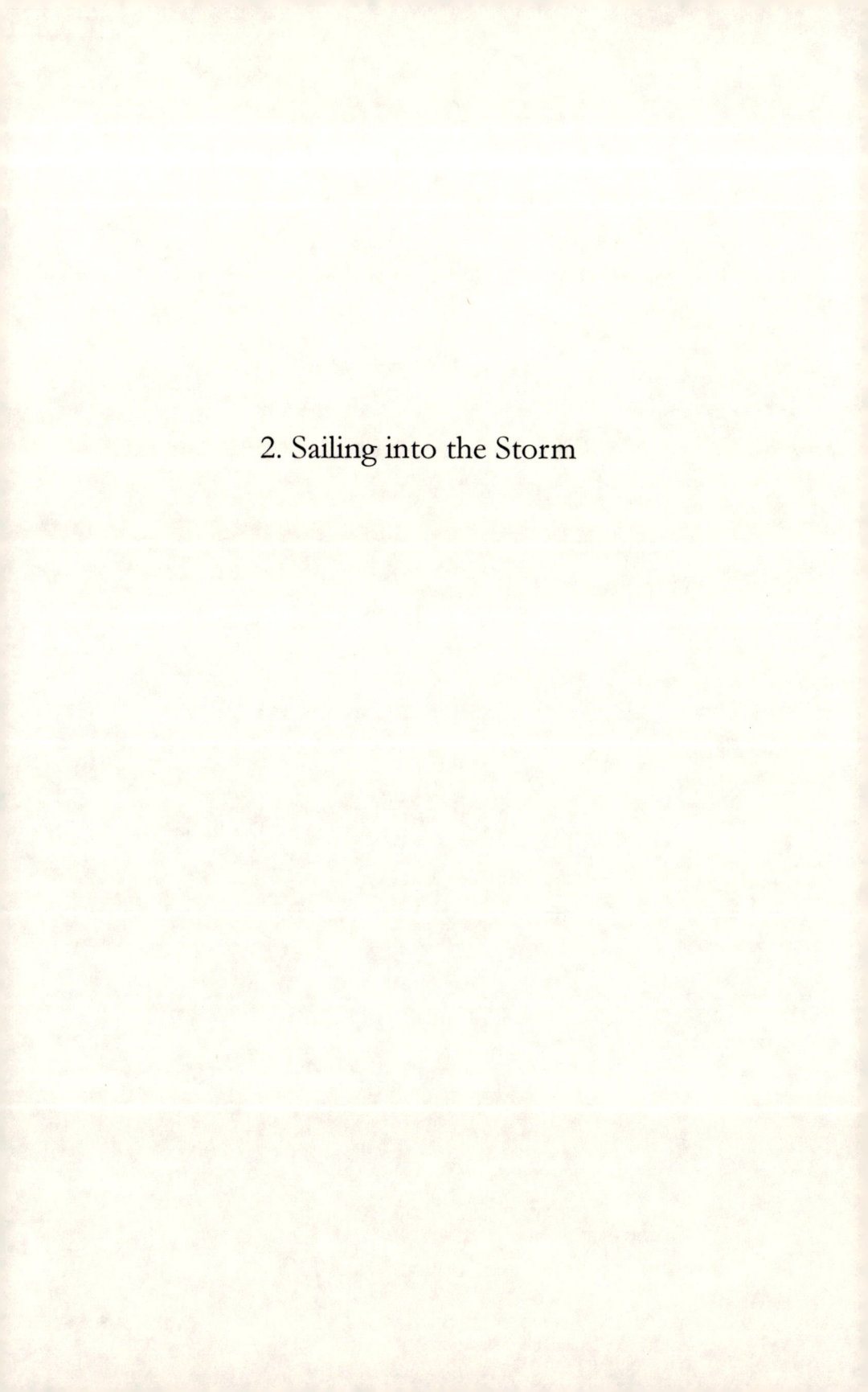

Curacao:
Notes from a Summer Memoir

I

The breakfast table basket was always filled with fruit—
    bananas, apricots, lemons, melons from the village

market. Long fronds of palms swayed in the breeze
    above us and a spray of salt water flavored every food

we tasted. We would watch as several sailboats strayed
    across the widest stretch of bay; birds' high-pitched

caws, like a killdeer's call, haunted us all that August.
    Repeated waves of heat seemed just as persistent.

Sun's glare appeared imperial, sovereign over everything:
    the pebbled beach beneath us pearled under its glaze.

II

Leaning over a small nearby hill, leaving a trail of gold
    along its shallow slope, even lazy light left on those

late afternoons converted the character of that landscape.
    But in evening comfort, daily warmth surrendered

to the busy night work of a trade wind and yellow lamps
    lit winding walkways like Japanese lanterns. A bistro

jazz band played Parker and Coltrane, those quicker
    saxophone notes mixing with the surf's own insistent

rhythm. We danced beside the sea, a slight swirl of sand
    rising in the moonlight like silver dust surrounded us.

Wharf at Sunset: A Sketch

A whole grove of masts wavers overhead
    as all the harbor boats already berthed

for night, dockside lines knotted to posts,
    rise slightly and then settle back with each

slow roll of sea swell. Even those few
    fishermen still lingering along the open

throat of the bay float closer to shore.
    Patiently awaiting the promised approach

of an evening storm, only a lone sailboat
    resists the urge to return, as a growing

current of air gathers in its fully unfurled
    panels. When we near the pier, we see

where a spread webbing of mesh strips
    has been placed beside the waterfront, gill

nets draped over poles and drying under
    this low late-day sun seemingly weary

after angling across another arc of sky.
    We thread our way through the sprawl

of gear and bait baskets that now lie
    scattered on the dock in clumps like little

islands of debris. The sorting has begun:
    barrels of bluefish, sea bass, flounder,

and perch dot the deck. Trash catch
    tossed overboard, gulls glide above us,

their wings tilted against a gusting wind,
    the sheen of their feathers glistening

and suddenly silken each time they turn
    toward the horizon and dip into the sea.

Triptych:
Fly-by over the Wildlife Refuge

I

When we first saw the F-4, nothing more
    than a pair of pitched wings glinting

like mica in the late daylight, and heard
    the sure exhaust of its twin engines roar

over the refuge, this entire peninsula sky
    blossomed with a white blur of birds

in flight as if someone somehow had
    suddenly shaken loose and tossed aloft

those new blooms of early spring already
    flourishing in fields flowing around us.

II

Even as that jet scratched its signature
    against the sky, and pointed off shore

toward the gridded platform of a carrier
    flight deck somewhere past the sea line,

we could see the slow, certain settling
    back of the flock, every whir and flutter

once again stilled, fixed in place among
    the landscape's many possessions as if

each pallid figure were no more than a fresh
    brush stroke restored to a darkened artwork.

III

Rimmed by hills covered with twisted
    vines and tough undergrowth of tangled

brush, a sandy margin of shoreline absorbs
    the afternoon's slanting sunlight. All along

the inlet, peaks of taller trees bend in the sea
    breeze as if to gesture toward crater dunes

and warmer pastures that lie behind their
    windbreak. Over the ocean, only a pale wisp

of vapor trail tails off into the distance,
    disappears above the deeper blue of open waters.

Sailing into the Storm

At first, the glassy surface of the sea
    seemed to gleam under an unending sun.

Large canvas sails hung loose
    like crepe. Then the wind rose slowly,

blowing easily about the hull,
    taking shape in the bright sheets, swelling

jib and spinnaker, seeping through
    the weeds along the shore, increasingly

leaping across the shallow waters
    until a sudden chill filled the channel.

Dark scars of clouds started to mar
    the skies over those far-off sandbars

that parallel the coastal shoulder,
    giving it a perceptive sense of definition,

of danger. As if weightless, gulls
    glided, their long white wings slightly

inclined, subtly rising, sweeping
    upward under influence of gale currents.

Soon, crowds of mottled clouds clotted
    the whole horizon, offering more evidence

of the approaching storm. Walls
    of squalls pinwheeling in, strong headwinds

swiftly crossed the sound, as we aimed
    the ship's prow toward the now-blackened

dock stationed just past a jutting
    peninsula tip, its piers pressed against

the rocky edge of a distant isthmus.
    Finally, we found protection beyond a jetty

projecting past the island's harbor,
    and although at last we felt safe, each

windswept spray of ocean left a taste
    of salt that lasted deep into a sleepless night.

Leaving Lisbon After a Lengthy Visit

I

When we departed, the ocean was
    as dark as wine, stars petaled the sky.

Sailing for home, our ship's wake
    trailed into the distance like a long

forefinger pointing back at that failing
    image of the Portuguese coast slowly

fading from view, as if by its indicating
    the way from which we had just come

we would somehow be urged to hasten
    our return to this dwindling peninsula.

II

Beyond the bow, toward the Azores,
    blackness was unending: nothing

but an unseen mist of sea air blowing
    cold over everyone on deck, concealing

the course ahead, as though the world
    we once knew now no longer existed—

perhaps had disappeared into the depths
    of those rolling waters roiling below

the hull—and it was hidden forever
    in thickening fog drifting before us.

Rainbow over Snow-Covered Landscape

It seemed no more than a smear across
    our frosted windshield as we approached

the bridge. Entering from somewhere
    beyond those rolling snowy slopes ahead,

it reached nearly all the way down to solid
    ponds that dotted the vast farms fast sliding

by us. But when we drove that dark arc
    of roadway that rose over the river, suddenly

we saw one distinct loft of light opposite
    an early afternoon sun, as if the heavens had

been stunned by some overlapping series
    of looping brush strokes and then a perfect

curvature of watercolors had been left
    across a canvas already filled with the thick

drifts of this snow-covered landscape.
    Although we knew what we were watching

was only evidence of an easy exchange
    of vapor from earth to sky, a slow settling

in the atmosphere that would lead this
    natural cycle toward closure, the air above

distant hillsides appeared dyed bright,
    dabbed with rich pigments. Even the wide

valley cupped underneath showed through
    translucent dapples of tint; for as far as we

could see, a slender blend of splendid
    hues now drew us toward the other shore.

Winter Nightfall in a Seaside Village

I

Above the bay, snow bleaches the hills
    where they rise right into a drift of cloud

cover. Even the lower crescents of terraces
    that rim the coast are now powdered white.

Throughout the village, chimney smoke
    blows about madly. All the flags along

the marina snap in the wind, sounding
    as sharp as those rifle-range shots on any

summer afternoon. Already, the lamps
    are coming on in one window after another.

II

As the day retracts its light, invites
    still colder weather, from the warmth

of our bedroom the whole ocean inlet
    opens before us like a natural pavilion,

its shoreline nearly ringing the black
    waters below and netting the darkness.

Surging gusts moan through the eaves
    and bend bared branches of seasonal trees

scraping the rooftop, as the escaping sap
    of fresh-cut wood sighs in our fireplace.

Easter Weekend: Sunrise by the Bay

I

Sunrise rubs its colors across slim clouds
      riding along the horizon as a stiff line of pines

is defined, their picket tops still ink-black
      against a brightening backdrop of daybreak.

Nearly as intimate and tactile as changing
      arrangements in the sky on any of Pissarro's

late quayside landscapes, a layer of haze,
      gray mixed with ochre, appears above the bay,

then begins to dissipate. It lifts like the blue
      wood smoke now drifting slowly in a light sea

breeze, blowing over those few homes
      with newly-lit windows beside this curved

surface of shorefront turning into the wind,
      curling like a thin fishhook toward the point.

II

Last year of a decade at the end of a century,
      end of the millennium, we are here for Easter

weekend. Most of the wildflowers already
      come to life, almost every one of them has begun

to unfold, each bud opening like a cupped
      hand hoping to hold whatever water or sunlight

the sky might have chosen to dole out.
    When we drove from home, more than six inches

of snow still filled the frozen cornfields
    around our house with windblown drifts raised

into waves by cold Canadian currents.
    But when warmer air arrives later this afternoon,

we know a golden glare will show over
    those Gulf Stream waters now barely stirring.

III

Below our hotel window, strands of wet
    sand will glint as if some silver spool of spun

thread suddenly had come undone
    under the sinking sun. We always revisit

this seaside in spring. We greet each
    morning here with relief, if not our belief

in salvation, as fruit trees—peach and cherry—
    renew themselves in the early blaze of these

lengthening days. Even the deepening
    green of front yards and the perennials

preening in gardens along the inland side
    of an ocean drive seem evidence presented

to persuade us we belong among them,
    as if they are offering us invitations to stay.

3. Fault Line

Revision by Lamplight

*Images are not quite ideas,
they are stiller than that . . . .*
—Robert Hass

Most of my time I've spent trying to find
    ways to state natural facts about abstract

thoughts with word images on a page,
    knowing to save only those ideas I felt

at least I needed. Then, late at night
    under lamplight when reading aloud

what lines I have written, I listen for their
    lessons I still seem incapable of learning—

hoping to obtain the wisdom I desire.
    Instead, I always seem to find myself

distracted while revising, seeing again
    another language present its sentence

with something as simple as the rhythm
    of rainfall or a whisper of wind outside

my window, where aligned hundred-watt
    bulbs of house security lights are now

shimmering and shining up from those
    shallow puddles offering their own bright

reflections as guides in the dark, replacing
    this night sky's far array of missing stars.

Envying the Art of the Cartographer

I

Late on another winter day in Indiana, lake water
    whitens under a slant of sunshine seeping beneath

scraps of clouds tacked against that bright backdrop.
    One more time, I am away from home, driving by

on a two-lane blacktop as a line of daylight again
    tightens along the horizon before tipping to twilight.

Soon, this low sky closing overhead will grind
    its way toward nightfall. I always ride with my camera

pack beside me—everything else I need stuffed
    into that fat sack of clothes in the back seat. Though

I may know how many of those roadside motel rooms
    or truck-stop diners I've seen this week, I doubt

I could count how many small towns I have traveled,
    each main street now replaced by a county highway.

II

When I photograph the landscape, I usually frame
    my shot so no telephone poles or power-line towers

will ever appear. I like photos of livestock in summer,
    lolling under a lone oak in the middle of a meadow,

or sycamores rising in sunlight, their shadows as long
    and rich as spring streams trickling toward a distant

river. I admire the Indiana paintings of Steele—beech
    trees leaning beneath the weight of snow or an amber

slant of autumn hillsides. My pictures of Lake
    Michigan cut out steel factories or the electric plant's

steam silos, as I often must edit the world before me.
    But on this trip I have decided to eliminate my desire

to filter. Instead, I now have chosen to show how slow
    erosion of human interference has altered all we see.

    III

Even my map, its folded-over creases rubbed almost
    to ripping and smudged by a greasy thumb print

just beneath a hunched bend of the Wabash River,
    seems as worn as that landscape sliding by my car

and about to fade into the gray atmosphere of dusk
    already as dark as August dust rising from a rutted

country lane. The photographs I've taken during
    this tour—a rotting hill of landfill, those foaming

suds flowing slowly from old pipes into clean creek
    water, rust-wrecked machinery clotting industrial lots,

Budweiser beer framed on a rented billboard blotting
    out a river view, four poor women sleeping overnight

side-by-side for warmth in a courthouse square—
    aren't the kind of pictures I'd find on any postcards.

IV

Sometimes, envying the art of the cartographer, I wish
    I had his ability to add a dash of color to landscape,

to make it the way he would want it to appear. I would
    like to locate place names between county boundaries

and beside the empty circles of cities sitting like tiny
    haloes alongside wavy fine hairs of state highways

or the winding twines of rivers. My font style or size
    would be discreet, of course, and oceans would be

the translucent blue of sapphire. I'd be sure to draft
    vast areas of lush hues to represent those last few

ranges of terrain marred only by dark suture
    scars of railways. My world would be made of neat

arrangements, taut designs of coastline or mountains
    drawn into a formal order that always stays the same.

Moonrise over the River

Following that thin embroidery of lights
    outlining a pedestrian footpath as it arches

across the waterway, we finally find ourselves
    alone at mid-river. Two small boats float by,

slipping nearly unseen into the darker distance
    toward a trestle bridge, its clattering procession

of black boxcars spanning the gap. Lines
    of pines conform to each twist of the river's

course, and tonight the tops of those trees
    are arrowing a starless sky, as though they

represent no more than a repetition of pickets
    fencing off the rest of the world. Appearing

as if that solid lid of night has been left
    unlatched, the narrow crescent of a new moon

rises into a cloud break over the horizon,
    sowing its slight seeds of whiteness. Pale light

covers the valley like a fresh linen cloth,
    much the way each year we have seen winter's

first layer of porous snowfall accumulate
    until all the ground around us is concealed.

However, tonight's sudden moonlight now
    unveils everything before us, even this secret

thread of current flowing ever so swiftly
    downstream, as tight stripes of whitewater

reveal the river's intricate stitching
    of seams through boulders or along those

smoother stones shining like knife blades
    sharpened for centuries against the water's edge.

Nocturnal:
Fayette County, West Virginia

> *All water shines down out of Heaven,*
> *And the things upon shore that I love*
> *Are immortal, inescapable, there.*
>   —James Dickey

Somewhat south of here, where the long,
    winding line of an interstate now strings

together those small nineteenth-century
    ore towns once built beside railroad routes

and waterways, the untroubled river tonight
    illuminated by moonlight still lies like just

another forgotten train track stretching
    into the distant hush accompanying each

evening that comes with its wide and blind
    presence, arriving as if brimming the black valley

with a cold molded cast of iron. All autumn,
    teeming leaves have floated over this river,

swarming across its narrow waters. Swept
    in its soft motion—past a few deserted coal

stations or under the untraveled Chesapeake
    and Ohio trestles—they follow the current's

shining surface downstream, the upper
    branches of their trees again seeded with stars.

Awaiting the Afternoon Rain

It is difficult to believe a place like this still
    exists. The warm lake water lies motionless,

arced against the land, curved like a camera
    lens, disturbed only by those ducks that slap

at the calm surface and shuffle onshore
    to cluster beside us, to accept our offerings

of bread crust. All around us, the pine trees
    tilt up the slopes, as if every one were leaning

under an unseen weight. Their limbs reach
    out toward one another, the longer branches

brushing each other in the upper air currents.
    Now clouds are pressing themselves against

ridge crests. Arching over the western edges,
    allowing only the last thin shafts of afternoon

sunlight to shine through, the storm front's
    violet striations have just begun to curtain

the canyon. A distant hiss of rainfall finally
    arrives, fast passing down the mountainsides

until a visible line is sighted, sliding toward us
    like a fine filter of translucent glass. The ducks

take flight, and all the images we have been
    watching before us fade slightly out of focus.

Lightning Strike

Long after the last rain, the hills were still
    filled with fire. Flames flowered along each

ridge. Every flare unraveled into a haze
    of ash. Coils of smoke rose over the river

basin. Rolling in the shifting winds,
    they climbed toward an indifferent sky

now merely powdered with those final
    few showering clouds futilely about to drift

out of the valley and beyond the horizon.
    Already, the old growths are dead or dying,

dried first by the August heat and then
    in an early autumn drought. One coal-dark

canyon brim carries its burn-scar
    far into an increasing blaze of sunlight,

rekindled with this late-morning clearing.
    Foothills fueled by scrub brush, several

winding lines of fire remain, filing down
    an incline, sifting through the upper thickets

like a cluster of summer streams tracking
    a single slope pillared with silver fir or sugar

pine and descending toward some distant
    ravine. By noon, new blossoms, as if sun-fed,

begin to appear, flashing their color against
    those stoked splotches of darker heights,

charred and smoldering. Safely away,
    sipping tea, we watch from under the shade

of our umbrella awning as this hotel verandah
    becomes cluttered with the luggage of other

visitors awaiting the arrival of an afternoon
    bus. Although we do not speak, feeling

any remarks we might make would seem
    insignificant, we listen to the feverish whispers

around us—phrases of amazement at all we've
    witnessed, words of fear or warning as a few

more plumes waver over the lone roadway
    to the airport. Tonight, when red sparks again

ignite, embroidering that black veil of hillside
    rising beside us, we will repeat these words.

Winter Waters:
White Mountains, New Hampshire

> *... a passing*
> *creekbed lies*
> *heaped with shining hills;*
> *and though the questions*
> *that have assailed us all day*
> *remain—not a single*
> *answer has been found . . . .*
>   —Mary Oliver

Late winter in this country every day seems
     like the last, overcast with gray columns of clouds.

Here, where the threads of runoff wishbone
     into one narrow creek—cold, clear, and quick—

a surface polish of ice covers everything,
     but nothing appears quite as slick and shiny

as those few frosted boulders deposited
     by a glacier ages ago, and now accompanied

by some glazed forms of birch trees bending
     among a grove apparently tired of standing

sentinel beside the water's path. Farther on,
     a ring of fir trees heavy with new snow surrounds

the mouth of this creek. High above,
     in the majestic crowns of these larger trees,

come the clatter and crackle of branches
     stunned by a sudden swirling in the persistent

winds that once again are carried across
    the nearby Canadian line, driven in from far-off

frontiers of northern Quebec. By now,
    the whole wooded hillside seems to be sealed

in a deep freeze, except for the scrawl
    of this one dark winding imprint—a thin stream

rolling over a series of shallow slopes.
    Gusts channel through treetops and wheel

about the upper crests. As the valley
    elbows, shifting snow packs—like sand dunes

beside a summer bay—gather on those small
    mound-banks marking this stretch of current.

Thick drifts curl around trunks or fallen
    limbs, are sculpted into abstract and unstable

shapes, adjusting position with each broken
    whirl of air flow. Afterwards, we notice a sense

of serenity, a calm that somehow seems
    to trail behind every storm's steady crawl across

this New England sky. In the same way
    we'd seen the Cape Cod shoreline often left smooth

by a late wave that crept down its tide-swept
    beach, each draft that reaches through these trees

leaves its handiwork—levels the uneven
    distribution of accumulation in the hollow below

or corrects the minor imperfections caused
    by a necklace of paw prints circling the lower

stream-pool into which this creek finally
      unspools. Wind-driven ridges of fresh snowfall

spread out from this hub like broken spokes.
      These seams extend irregularly, bending toward

the stillness of those woods wrapped around
      us, mingling only with winter's motions of wind

and water, until they disappear into drifts
      of darkness that lap at the edges of this opening.

Fault Line:
A Farewell in Five Fragments

*Until we were what we must have wanted to be:
shapes the shapelessness was taking back.*
—Jorie Graham

I

All afternoon, in silence, we've been following
    another hidden edge of earth, an ancient

break in terrain where tremors once rumbled
    underground; but this morning the quiet

we had sought was broken only by songs
    of sparrows or the rare call of a cardinal.

II

Earlier, opposite one another, a dark pair
    of harrier hawks hovered above us;

then they banked and whirled in an increasing
    swirl of air, exchanging place with every

turn, each concentric and quickening ring
    merely a replica of the circle drawn before.

III

In the valley, long arms of a willow wrestled
    with this lifting wind and an overhanging

branch still heavy with leaves moved in a perpetual
    stir of stream water; soon, we saw a whole

slope of quaking aspen, their heart-shaped leaves
    going gold under the slant of autumn sun.

IV

Although we know this fault line is nothing more
    than a simple split in the geologic plate,

it seems endless as it tracks across that great sprawl
    of nature before us—one length of landscape

pulled apart and reassembled, raised and wrinkled
    like the gathered pleat on a large garment.

V

Here, where thunder once rose with those hazel
    hills now entering this changing sky

before us, gray and weighted by rain, we listen
    to the shrill, distant whistling of a freight train;

we await the approaching storm, still wishing
    we could hear that softer caroling of sparrows.

4. Constellations over Colorado

Canyon Tributary

I

Throughout the canyon, a vast veinwork
    of shallow streams still descends, tentatively

trickling toward this chilly rivulet—snow-melt
    tumbling over rock slides, lurching through wild

floral growths and weeds. Its embankment
    is edged with scrawny trees still tilting away

from a western wind—their limbs hunched
    roughly under one another in awkward clusters,

the shadows of their little leaves gathered
    along the ground like thousands of black beads.

II

On higher terrain, where earlier we had
    watched a file of white-tail deer as they disappeared

over a ridge line, we now can see how many
    tangled acres already have dried and strangled

in scrub brush. Just above us, the sun
    continues its slow shuttle across a cloudless sky.

By late summer drought, some of these slopes
    will be veiled with smoke rising from the severe fires

that flare each year. Scarves of dark clouds will
    unfold over the hillsides, enclosing the valley below.

III

Although this gorge open before us appears
    no greater than a thin suture scar on most maps,

a mere seam stuck somewhere between two
    counties, every time we've come it has begun

to mean much more. Here alone, we are able
    to take delight in the odd disorder of everything.

Yet, someway, each day we return to the safety
    at home—in any weather, no matter what changes

occur. Falsely, we arrive; like deceptive images
    of distant fixed stars, we seem to stay the same.

IV

Already on this hot afternoon, traveling the narrow
    length of the canyon floor still mud-soft with winter's

waters, we acknowledge our desire for security,
    our need to follow these gentle currents coursing

toward town. We also are aware that those few
    waning tracts of shrubs and wildflowers will not last

much longer. Even from these deepest recesses,
    soon the sun's strength will drain any remaining

evidence of life. Back in the valley, we will begin
    our secret vigil—await the bleak and billowing skies.

Mountain Meadow:
Night Climb After a Storm

> *Now I limp on, knowing*
> *the moon strides behind me* . . . .
> —James Wright

I

Following the fine line of a flashlight
    beam, we find ourselves alone, groping

our way into this opening among wooded
    crests, and all around us suddenly seems

to awaken when that nightly slide of stars
    again starts shining against the dark sky.

II

As the moon, too, now moves once more
    past its black background like some large

lantern carried across a broad field, brightens
    the entire expanse of meadow before us,

we're newly reminded how easy it would be
    to forget everything we have left behind.

Spring Morning:
Descending an Abandoned Mountain

These sleek trees, like thin anchor lines
    that scar the sands of a crowded inlet as they hold

old boats from one another, fade
    from view slowly in snowdrifts. On lower slopes

the whole terrain is wooded and hard,
    twisted trees shine darkly like expensive leather,

wet, rubbed with oil. The river widens,
    swollen by snow-melt, floods the one road long

forgotten by loggers, as the risen
    mist surrenders the foothill forest, uncovers

red ripples of trails, which once extended
    to mining camps in the valley. The clearing reveals

a clutter of gravestones at the edge
    of an opening that had shown sheltered rows

of low-roofed cabins and a company lodge
    where many men were quartered whose names

no one any longer knows. In each sudden
    shower of early sunlight, the smooth white surfaces

of these slabs flush brightly; forever,
    they flash their anonymous and dateless planes.

Winter Scene: After the Aneurysm

Snow was falling slowly over black ovals
    of ponds, clouds already having drained

even these pools of moonlight. A distant
    fog drifted across the darkness of farmlands

and above that fringe of fir trees beyond
    the large barn that now wore its own coat

of snow like a fresh whitewash glossing
    its flaws, an overlay softening each angle

of its architecture or, like a supple brushwork,
    somehow smoothing every uneven substance.

Before long, the whole snow-covered surface
    seemed to roll easily, linking objects together

as if they'd sought support from one another.
    A glare of lamplight washed over my shoulder

as I watched this change of weather moving
    through. Everywhere, the elements seemed

to be settling into an arrangement of black
    and white, a scene that suddenly resembled

the colorless landscape in an Ansel Adams
    photograph. Yet, as this late wave of winter

dusted a plot of light outside our window
    so that it appeared brighter than it might,

the first drifts glistened like ground glass,
    sharpening those hard edges of shading

now outlined by the shape of the pane.
    As though I could know that night would

be like no other, I wondered if someday
    this image will be nothing more than

a memory lost in the haze of time gone
    by or part of a wish we had once hoped

would come true—and I thought about
    how drowsy with doubt we'd both become.

Wyoming Elegy

Stunned by the sun's brilliance, the heat
    now beating down on an ageless landscape,

we suffer in silence the state-wide
    drive. Love and death have lured us far along

this laser-straight highway as surely
    as each skater's blade leaves its precision

slit across the smooth, cool skin of ice
    atop a winter pond. There seems no distinction

between seasons any longer. Even
    the flare of sun still suspended somewhat

above the horizon appears misplaced,
    perhaps lost, tossed into position like a random

dab of paint on an abstract work
    of art. Nothing makes sense any more,

or at least that's what we believe.
    Your mother—betrayed by her own body,

her erratic life turned suddenly away—
    always nourished those whom she touched,

just as the twisting waters that wind
    along the length of this road feed the tall reeds

and blossoming shrubbery reaching out
    from the riverbanks, leaving only a narrow green

signature scrawled beside an interstate.
    Still, this little coloring seems enough amid

broad blank land that surrounds it.
    And so, too, we believe that one lasting image

is enough, know in future daydreams
    we will see her slow slope-shouldered figure

once again, tending to her garden
    flowers, stooping to admire their lovely shapes,

bending over them the way she'd
    always bow when in the presence of nature's

beauty—as if poised in reverent devotion.
    Once more, we'll watch as she walks that path

through the greenhouse that kept all
    her treasures safe in those most bitter months

of winter. And yet, today only one
    thing matters: somewhere under the enormous

summer sky of Wyoming spreading
    over everything, where even this wild river

threading its way through the moonscape
    territory before us soon will have begun to run

dry, that woman, who once knew how to love
    all the small wonders of her world, now lies still.

After Leaving the Hotel

> *. . . we learn how our own history has its exits*
> *and its entrances, its waning phase.*
>   —Amy Clampitt

    I

Late in a day yet tainted by rain clouds as dark
    as slate and still swiftly drifting in a distant

wind on the horizon, when pools of water runoff
    from overflowing gutters lay in the shadings

at our feet like fading grease stains or even
    abstract shapes of black paint framed by those

same gray pavement blocks one might find
    anywhere in this city, somewhat numbed

by the cold, but unaware of its full effect,
    we waited outside a subway station across

from the hotel for the cabs we had called,
    and if we ever spoke at all, it was only

of that wet weather or the careless way
    everyone else tried to rush by. Somewhere

beneath a sidewalk grating, the muted rumble
    of a delayed train slowly rolled below traffic

headlights on yellow taxis and buses stuttering
    along the avenue, while street lamps and neon

signs above storefronts or a café window
    also were just greeting the arrival of dusk.

II

Some clumsy Christmas shoppers stumbled
    past us, nearly toppling over—each one

weighted down by an apparently painful
    arrangement of large, flat packages underneath

others perhaps the size of small birdcages—
    as if engaged in a strange new dance. I know

at that moment I would've wanted to imagine
    one of the romantic New York City vistas

in Woody Allen's films filled with characters
    whose ordinary lives are all choreographed

to Gershwin, guided through black-and-white
    scenes that seem to be sketched onto the screen

as much as any charcoal artwork chosen
    for a museum wall. I could have envisioned

an image of a bridge over the river at nightfall—
    its span lit by an arc of bright lights shown

rising and falling like stars showering down
    from twinkling tips of holiday sparklers waved

overhead by children, its whole suspension
    doubled on dark, slow-flowing waters below.

III

But it's plain to see, nothing I might have
    created in my mind could have changed

either the truth we then knew enough
    to acknowledge or the way faint remains

of that dank day have lingered in my memory.
    Today, as I think of those stray moments

that have stayed with me all these years—
    endured like my father's old clothes,

well-worn suits or plaid sports coats
    and wide-striped ties yet kept hanging

in a guest bedroom closet, but belonging
    only to another era that had ended long ago—

I now know our odd absence of pain
    and the cold we both noticed on that last

afternoon, suddenly stunted by an early
    darkness, followed by the feelings of loss

and regret we still appear to share are no
    more than normal emotional costs a couple

might expect after reflection upon leaving
    the site where their love's come undone.

Constellations over Colorado

I

Stars sharpen, again outlining the great shapes
    of those constellations marking that far

sky yet resting what little weight it may offer
    upon the slopes of this dark landscape.

II

Just above a cluster of aspen along one ridge,
    tonight's gibbous moon is now rising

like an ivory fan spread open as a last resort,
    a way to wave away this summer heat.

III

When a brief river breeze presses at the edges
    of those trees all around this redwood

deck, their leaves seem to whisper, as if trying
    to find a word or two of consolation.

IV

An endless murmur carries on with its rumors
    in the gully beneath me where a current

moves past, staggers through those small stones
    sifting this river for thousands of years.

V

Sometimes I wonder if I might try to decipher
    their language, but to do so would be

futile, almost as useless as searching for advice
    under astrological signs of a horoscope.

VI

The candlelight flickers on this wooden table,
    even appears to give a knowing wink,

as I now look out at the back of that black forest
    across those slow-flowing waters below.

VII

Just after sunset, when you had left, the horizon
    was sprinkled with that spray of daylight

that always lingers a little longer, as if it is still
    hoping to hold on to what's already lost.

VIII

Later, by midnight, even though everything may
    lie under the artful display of that sky

petaled with patterned starlight, I am waiting
    for some other sign that will not come.

IX

At a time like this, when every bit of evidence
    we need of perfection locks into position

and I see the ordered world before me, I know
    there is no use seeking any alternative.

X

I watch the moon and stars, each in its charted
    spot, as that lunar light reaches through

treetops, washes over the large logs and dark
    stumps fit into this lodge's architecture.

XI

Beside one another, Cassiopeia and Andromeda
    keep me company even in their distance,

and when that flame wavers a last time, I believe
    I might find relief writing these final lines.

XII

But I know tomorrow, when that first pale flag
    of sunrise unfurls, the night will surrender

its tight grip over this valley, and even those few
    far figures of stars also will wander away.

Listening to Lester Young

> ... *regrets are always late, too late!*
> —John Ashbery

Late at night, I'm listening to one of Lester Young's
    slower solos again, and although I know he's playing

those same notes I've heard over and over, as the tone
    of his tenor saxophone turns toward a lower register,

even that patter of cold drizzle now pasting shadowy
    leaves against my window seems to follow his lead.

I wonder what you would be doing tonight and I want
    to write a few lines in my notebook about how blue

and ivory skies gave way to rain today after you left,
    how coming home from the train station, I thought

I saw something, a large and ominous animal suddenly
    outlined by lightning on that sparsely wooded hillside

beside the deserted highway we always drive to save
    a little bit of time. As you travel farther away, hurry

through the muted darkness still surrounding everything,
    so that you cannot even see the land tilting at the sea

or the gulls slanting overhead when you approach
    the coastline, I imagine you beginning a new book

in the dim light of that passenger car, reading another
    long novel about characters not so unlike ourselves,

each chapter titled and numbered as if to indicate life's
    merely a neat progression of unpredictable episodes.

By tomorrow evening you will be at that old hotel
    where we once stayed for days in a room overlooking

plaza monuments deformed and whitened like marble
    by a winter storm, while its foot of snowfall closed

the city down as though no one there had ever known
    such weather in their lives. If you were still here,

you'd be able to hear Lester backing Billie Holiday
    on another ballad recorded more than six decades

ago, but years before the two of them finally knew
    the truth about that high cost of living they would

have to pay. I'm beginning to believe their duets of lost
    love, ways they phrase each line of lyric or melody,

create images in the mind as vivid as any photo
    or poem we might have seen, evoke those places

Prez and Lady Day played in their earlier days—
    Harlem cabarets and late-night cafés downtown,

or those small neighborhood halls with bare walls
    and a gray haze of smoke above the stage, the ebony

and violet glow of an angled piano lid under indigo
    lights, and a congregation of friendly faces gradually

fading into the black background with a persistent
    chatter and clatter of glasses that lets everyone know

they are not alone. In the half hour before your
    departure, when we sat silently on that station

platform bench, as though any attempt at conversation
    would be hopeless and in fear someone around us

might overhear what we had to say, I tried somehow
    to take into account how far apart we already were:

even then, I felt regrets are all we had left in common.

5. Rafting the Rapids

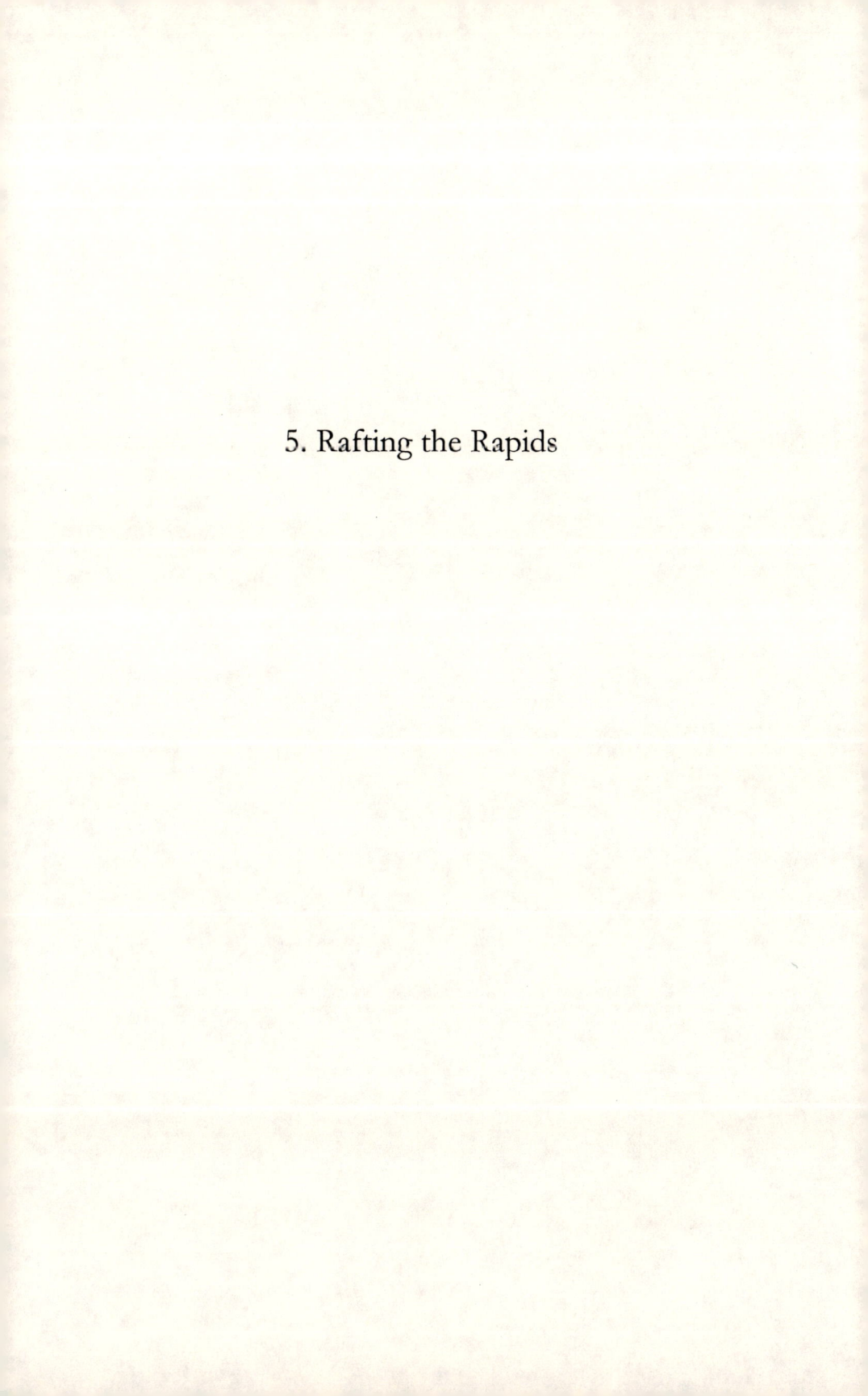

Invoking a Line by Wallace Stevens

> *... the seeming of a summer day ....*
> —Wallace Stevens

Just before dusk, the parched men and women
    begin drinking gin-and-tonics as they sit on porches

with white wicker chairs and ornamental planters
    still filled with wiry stalks of withered annuals.

Every evening, under the constant hum of insects
    and buzz or crackle of a bug lamp, their conversations

chronicle another summer drought. They speak
    about scenes that seem evidence of timelessness,

indifference, or rather more distressing, loss:
    how for weeks even a screen of storm clouds

could not cool the hot contours of those two lanes
    curving through this blistered countryside; how

for many mornings smoke drifting from brush
    fires blotted the distant sky; how otherwise each noon

horizon disappeared in glare like a bleached absence
    dotting the view on an overexposed photograph;

how by late afternoon a mirage of heat ripples
    would waver over bare asphalt at the drive-in diner;

or simply how the air was often empty of chirping
    birds that now stayed quiet all day as they perched

in patches of cross-hatch darkness under shade trees.

Spring Sunset:
Learning About the Death of a Friend

I

This morning when my wife and I were still
    planting spring flowers among others

yet wet with tears of dew glistening
    like jewels strewn in the sunshine,

we remembered drought and death a decade ago
    that had marred the year of our marriage.

II

Moving into the heart of noon heat,
    a lone crow rose above the patios

and mown lawns of neighbors' homes.
    It flew low over our yard and broke

the silence, calling in a repetitive pattern like rote
    memory with its coarse and mournful caw.

III

As late afternoon edges toward evening
    and that golden halo of sunset starts

to fold itself into some distant hills, black
    bands of shade have begun to show,

imposing shadows lengthening over everything,
    displacing that greater brilliance of daylight.

IV

A blur of blue dusk, its vague veil rising
    like smoke, eventually replaces

that glare of earlier hours with a rough
    smudge of darkness until even this

familiar landscape around us suddenly becomes
    unrecognizable and vanishes into an absence.

V

Despite the night, while we sleep, I know those
    new blooms will reappear under moonlight

as if candlelit—flashing the way windblown
    flames from a minor fire might flare

or blazing like little lanterns left behind as gifts
    to illuminate all in the garden around them.

Summer Evening: Truro, 1947

> *I have never been able to paint
> what I set out to paint.*
> —Edward Hopper

Sometimes, I never consider putting figures in
    until I actually start painting:

none ever appears in their preparatory sketches.
    I'd prefer to leave them out.

As an illustrator, I was always taken by archaic
    shapes of architecture or remnants

of ancient nature, but the editors wanted fiction—
    people placed on the page, waving

their arms about. And even today, as late summer
    rain again blurs these scraps

of landscape that now fill our window—the sprawl
    of pasture, thickening grassland

spilling toward those low rolling hills beyond
    a shallow pond—I also think

once more of an earlier August night in Nyack,
    though not so very long ago,

and how those lovers I thought I saw embracing
    on a neighbor's lawn remain,

somewhat vaguely in my faulty recall, shaded
    beneath wind-shaken limbs

of an old oak, while its serrated silhouette is still
    traced distinctly in my mind

against an implausible light of stars yet drifting
    across a moonless sky. If only

truth were so easy to depict with such details;
    nothing I know, I can assure

you, is really like the scene I remember here.
    Instead of invented narratives,

I'd hope viewers notice contrast caused by sunlight
    brightening an empty room,

the bleaching of a beachfront cottage facade
    under summer's noonday flare,

or the softening of solid objects during dusk.
    Thus, I must mix imagination

with any of my memories. I find, in working,
    always the disturbing intrusion

of elements not a part of my most interested
    vision. So, I will fill this spare

setting the way I often have before: the couple
    are now outside a closed door

and caught in another conversation that cannot
    be heard by anyone else; each

leans back supported by a front porch ledge;
    the bare floor of this porch

is squared by glare of an overhead light forming
    corners; the horizontal slats

of stark white siding are sliced by sharp lines edging
    a window sash or door frame;

twin entrance columns are darkened, wedged
    in shadow; the walkway approach

to the porch steps is lost in nightfall's black border.
    After all is done, some may say

the young woman in this painting appears unhappy
    or reluctant and the young man

seems to be offering an explanation or attempting
    persuasion, that these two represent

tension and express discontent we've all experienced.
    But I know none of this is true.

Although others can endlessly speculate about
    the troubled lives of both figures,

their personal story was not a real concern for me
    nor what I most wanted to show.

It is an exercise in composition and form: merely light
    streaming down, the night all around.

Cross Sections: Notes from a Memoir

    I. *Wildwood Crest, New Jersey: 1965*

That summer, the last one before our own home
        in the city was sold, we stayed for weeks at a favorite

uncle's old New Jersey cottage beside the sea,
        its salt-blistered pinewood siding painted slate gray

with slight lines of white trim rising high above
        the Atlantic on a bluff covered by clusters of bayberry

bushes or dune shrubs and the stubble of scrub
        brush. Although left as a gift, much of the lush

garden—flowers he'd cultivated and grown
        during years since returning from war, wounded

in Normandy by machine-gun fire from a ridge
        bunker—had shrunken and many of the perennials

had been neglected after his death, still a few
        groups of blue delphinium bulged beside knots

of red poppies yet bobbing on their long stems
        in the light sea breeze like tiny boats anchored

against a gulf current. Lying on a hammock
        in a sprawl of shade and silence beneath the only

pair of pin oaks to be found anywhere around,
        I had often imagined escape, crossing that grand

expanse of ocean then opening before me below
        a glaze of sunlight as if its quiet waters had suddenly

been placed under taut cellophane or maybe even
        thin fabric interwoven with an overlay of silver lamé.

    II. *Le Havre, France: 1984*

I know there may be no way for me to explain
        what exotic images I expected that I might find

upon arriving at the shore on the opposite side,
        or to share how strongly I felt my longing to hear

those languages spoken there. But almost two
        decades later when I walked alone along another

beach cliff, its rocky crest looming over a bare
        and bending stretch of narrow coastline ninety miles

west of Paris, suddenly shadowed by clouds
        just then crowding out a rust-red sun setting

behind the blur of a motorboat and, though
        farther off beyond darker blue of harbor waters,

murky outlines of cargo ships floating past
        like those wide designs—black blocks of brush

strokes—that sweep across a Franz Kline canvas,
        again I thought of summer as a boy by the shore

north of Cape May: I remembered days filled
        with scenes which only now seem to mean so much

more than when I first lay in that hammock
        near the edge of the seaside at high tide, the lazy

bay brightening before me. I heard the sigh
        of backwash as each wave receded from the sea

ledge, and I listened to those lonesome oaks,
    their twisted branches this time alive with birdsong.

Rafting the Rapids

I

In August, under noonday haze, the valley fills
    with small fields of wildflowers. The morning

mist has long since risen above this basin
    and begun to wind its way uphill, fog still

hugging high fire roads that twist toward stark
    ridge tops. Even early lines of dark clouds

that appeared at dawn have finally cleared.
    Now, as we follow the river's scrawled signature

across this country, floating rafts past hillsides
    spattered with patches of spruce, pine, and fir,

we can see how these steep slopes quickly climb
    right into the open sky, its bright horizon clipped

only by an uneven outline of rim rock. Here,
    where the current's flow slows to a lazy pace

and tawny silt stains the river until detailed
    beneath the glare of midday blaze it takes on

the color of tea, we wade cool waters still chilled
    by late winter's snow as we drift downstream.

II

We await the rumble of rapids before heading
    for a few watershed buttes just beyond the next

bend where the faster whitewater is running.
       As the afternoon sun starts its descent, we move

gently toward a narrow sluice, shoot through
       a sudden drop, then surge over those bedrock holes

and rolling wave trains swollen with the seasonal
       release flushed from an upriver dam.   By sunset,

we have slipped past the last falls of the gorge:
       all that's left is one short stretch of mild ripples

and a small section of beach for landing. Tonight,
       we will lie beside this constant sweep of current,

that continues as persistently into the future as life
       itself, and fall asleep beneath a flood of darkness

marred merely by sparks embarking from some
       faraway stars scattered like moments of memories

we'd hoped to hold on to, those shattered fragments
       solely able to offer light from times already passed.

Coronary Thrombosis

Even when he skidded down that gravel drive,
    a lane rising as white in the late moonlight

as a snow-blown mountain trail in midwinter,
    and fled for who-knows-where, his old coat

thrown on in flight against an unseasonable
    chill and already smelling from a night-long

dribble of cheap, hard liquor, his head still
    filled with those foul thoughts that had been fed

by the soft, sweet talk of a barmaid he'd once
    held close in the shadows of a hotel room

(a woman whose whiff of perfume he had
    always embraced, but someone he no longer knew),

as he raced past the rows of damaged grain
    or sped alongside the erosion of those dull,

empty fields with topsoil now washed away
    by wind and rain, he must have just begun

to sense the clamp of that blood clot tightening
    inside him—his fingers numbing, as though

feeling the steering wheel through thick
    gloves; surely, despite any anger against this fate

he had been given, he must have hung on
    for life until the bottom rocks of that roadside

ravine suddenly glistened in the angled beams
    of headlights and spilled across his windshield

like some storm of meteorites suddenly appearing
 on the backdrop of a black horizon one summer

at midnight, though tossed toward Earth ages ago.

Solitude:
A Meditation in Four Fragments

> *O Solitude! if I must with thee dwell,*
> *Let it not be among the jumbled heap*
> *Of murky buildings; climb with me the steep—*
> *Nature's observatory . . . .*
> —John Keats

I. *Autumn*

This distant rhythmic clicking, boxcars traveling
      through these transparent precincts of another

quiet night—dark profiles against a blank
      horizon made milky with moonlight, moving

westward—also moves me, as I feel, though not
      for the first time, the happiness of anonymity.

II. *Winter*

I've often understood the need to be unnoticed,
      to witness the world without intrusion, as when

alone at home a wordless murmur of wind caws
      its hoarse call outside one's window, and glancing

past the garden gate one sights a scrawny herd
      of deer forced down from the snowy mountains.

III. *Spring*

This morning, the trees swelling with blossoms
      seem so much more. In the dimness of dawn even

dewdrops appear as silver spangles sewn into a great
        green broadcloth. I've been walking these woods

where no one has wandered all winter, sequestered
        deep beneath random slant of branches, content.

    IV. *Summer*

All along the lakefront, the afternoon shadows
        have finally fallen once more across this sandbar

where I have been wading. Even in this season,
        these waters quickly chill as if left as evidence,

an effort to remind me of their ancient glacial
        origins. I pause in praise of nature's legacy.

Nightfall After a Storm

*Sunset and evening star
And one clear call for me!*
—Alfred, Lord Tennyson

I

Each wedge of sunlight edges through
    this sky now crowded with clouds

suddenly incandescent, spreading
    lavish color, conferring blessing upon all.

II

The skeletal limbs of winter trees
    stir a cold north wind, offering clear

evidence of the storm's end,
    removing nightfall's final obstacles.

III

Stars surface, rearranging everything.
    The entire horizon is altered as we

glimpse far past the fast slide of dusk,
    a welcoming we might almost return.

Seeded Light is Edward Byrne's sixth collection of poetry. His works also have appeared in numerous literary journals—including *American Literary Review, American Poetry Review, American Scholar, The Literary Review, Mid-American Review, Missouri Review, North American Review,* and *Southern Humanities Review*—as well as an assortment of poetry anthologies. In addition, he has written essays for various critical texts, such as *Mark Strand* (Chelsea House), edited by Harold Bloom, and *Condition of the Spirit: the Life and Work of Larry Levis* (Eastern Washington University Press), edited by Christopher Buckley and Alexander Long. Byrne is a professor of American literature and creative writing at Valparaiso University, where he serves as the editor of *Valparaiso Poetry Review.*